THE WHISPERING KING

Falling asleep

Tears freshly rolling down my cheek

Pain of caring

Shame of sharing

Voices re-entering

Languidly declaring

Thoughts of treason

Ignoring reason

 Shadow of darkness

Snapshot capturing false charges

Man in a ghost town

Losing his sharpness

Isolation growing near

Fear of becoming heartless

Man of hate

Psychotic - lethargic

Man of peace

Whispering King - stoic

Poet gone unnoticed

He hangs

Cold - departed

People cared half-hearted

Leading back into the Ghost Town

Back where we had started

REPLACING FEARS

I woke up early that morning with the night still knocking at my door. Haunted and chased by the moon, I packed my bags and headed West. Though the desert will surely tell tales of its own sorrows - it will never know mine… As I arrived, the sun greeted me with a warm smile only to declare its own poison. The following day I watched the sun rise over a watery grave only to realize I've replaced my first fear with my last. Eternity truly is long. Hurry - forever will begin tomorrow… I have no where left to hide.

THE TRIBE

We walk the same stride

Sweet love of my life

Stalemate of eyes glaring

Immaculate - nothing comparing

Thoughts as high as the sky

Losing points of reference

Civilian contracts of destruction

Stale cold blue hell

Dark caves now for sell haphazardly

Perfect for societies shunning

Throughbreds we were hunting

Call of the wild at heart

Who is to join our tribe?

Only for the stunning

Riding in the distance-

I saw a pale horse coming

Devil's advocate

His face labyrinth

We were confused and scared

Stories for our children to tell

RECOGNIZED

Painfully recognized

The sweet beauty finally replied

Telling tales from our ancestors

Though none survived

We were forced to leave the tribe

Utterly,

Uncontrollably,

Terrified with what we saw

Our vision was dark blue,

Though far from frozen

Now here I lay in the day's shade

Forgotten thoughts rushing in

To pay me a visit

The tower bell rings signify

Yet another hour is missing

As if any of us could forget

LOST

Lost in the desert

Losing my faith

Starving and lonely

Get me out of this place

Remembering my daughters and wife

My only escape

My hearts still longing

To accept this fate

It's true I have an issue

But I can walk away

If quitting was an option

Addictions would be erased

Day two - I cracked

Got on my knees and prayed

Said if you get me out of here

I'll try to change my ways

The heavens opened up

I thought heard God say

Son you've been dead for years

Though it's never too late to be saved

Visions of heaven eclipsed my eyes

Visions of my life- thought I had died

Promises that was kept

His sons sacrifice

A message of faith

Inscrutable lines

As soon as this ended

Night arrived

Finding an oasis

Easily defined

There I stayed

Hoping they's find

THE PUDDLE

I can lie in fields

I can forget the rose

I can set us on fire

But I can never let go

This, however, I want to you to know

The puddle on the ground has been following us around

Just to remind us, it was he we crowned

The endless names that passed it by

Never seemed to let it dry

Because from all the chaos

No one will ever see

It was just the puddle -

Being too deep

It's just the puddle on the ground

It's seen this empty town

You can dive into its depths

But be careful not to drown

The puddle on the ground

Formed by falling rain

By rain I mean tears

Followed shortly by pain

In our hearts the puddle remained

Some things never change

BLACK LIVES MATTER

Damn right black lives matter

Malcom X

Martin Luther King Jr.

Rayshard Brooks

George Perry Floyd

Breonna Taylor

Alton Sterling

Sandra Bland

Tamir Rice

Michael Brown Jr

Eric Garner

Oscar Grant III

Just to name a few

When will the madness end

To live in a world judged by the color of our skin

It's a dark cloud over this realm

But still we press on

United we stand my brothers and sisters

For the future is bright

The young generation don't take shit from blacks or whites

FALLING STARS

As lights fade we'll fail to wait

These thoughts we love carry weight

So as we watch the stars collide

I'll see them fall beneath your eyes

As moments pass I am sure we'll be-

Another step closer to eternity

Does it hurt when your alive?

Do rivers flow when lies provid-

The truths we once believed

And what about the seas we swam across?

As once said:

"We will carry own cross"

Love and hate in time we'll find-

Such a very fine line

Was this all a famous quote?

A memory known that we once spoke

I lost my mind under the sky

Thought I'd wonder if you would cry

Does the snow fall when there is nothing more

Because I'm sure-

With eyes as bright as yours,

It's a lot easier to see-

The waves crashing below your feet

And even though I'm wrong

I'll never say I'm sorry

So I'll catch you on the moon,

To be the stars to fall at noon

DIE FOR HONOR

This moment has me thinking

Life is worth the beating

Though painful and deceiving

A pain worth feeling

I'm so happy that I'm here

God's Gift

Another day

Blessing me with a spear

A warrior dying before disgrace

Honor fills my spirit

Making my own fate

Washing sins off by the lake

No fear on my face

There is no other way

WHISPERING KINGS' FINAL APPERANCE

Death walks on the Ghost Town's highway

War Torn Master holding the keys

Refusing to set me free

Hiding behind my own imprisonment

The cage - watching intensely

The day,

Just now reaching its dawn

Sun using planets as pawns

No one left to understand coherent

Rome is burning now

Then again- what isn't

The Whispering King presents a challenge

Dragging behind him the fears of my past

The Lion Master,

Once a hero,

Now a new product of fear

The Whispering King,

Making his final appearance

Master roars as I am now watching fearlessly

Whispering King now speaking

Though not loudly

His voice carried with the wind

Filling empty

Yet his voice was heard over everything

I finally see…

The Master dropped the keys by my feet

I was freed

Thank you Whispering King

WAR TORN LION

The war torn lion

So misunderstood

He fought the questions Just to prove he could

Now he's all alone

A cage as his home

This beast might roar

But it's nothing more

He can no longer wage war as before

Day after day people will pass him and say

"Dad look at this one-

He isn't as proud in his cage"

The War Torn Lion

Hoping for the day to come-

When he can return to the wild

Chasing the rising sun

There are no more smiles

Traveling fearless

Maine long,

blood cold,

claws threatening

They're getting close,

His eyes begin to glow,

The deed is done,

No one to know

IGNORANCE - BLISS?

Writings always seem to reflect beginnings or ends

Where timeless tales revive the lives

The dead and forgotten

Where have the people of our time gone?

A time in our history based around wrong

Simple days and simple nights

Always fade cliche under stars lights

Flowing like a river,

Our majestic sea

When and where will my foes meet

Will they form plots against my family?

The change is destiny

Resulting in me

Watching the world burning

Right before my eyes,

All that's left now are ruins and golden lies

That majestic sea no longer flows as it should

Everything now so blatantly misunderstood

Confused by the cars that pass them by

Eyes fading away slowly

Writing poetry under the elm

I pray this vision last

Time may only tell my detachment

The only thing now that makes sense,

Ignorance- Bliss?

THE GREAT BIRTH: PEACE

Warmth of the sun touching skin

Ocean is just ahead,

No sorrow here

Sand instead

Perfect religions all agree on this

The ocean is beautiful

Simpatico

Though wars are still waged

For different believing

Peace on Earth

Worth pondering

Though hard conceiving

Would it not be a great birth?

It really shouldn't seem that absurd

In the end who wants to be hurt

Stop aborting

Start believing

It could happen,

With a little dreaming

UNWRAPPING FREEDOM

Freedom met me today

Brought me a new present

It was filled with all my favorite things

Taught me a new lesson

Be patient son

Always try to listen

Always make time for life

Always tell what you're feeling

When you are on the highest rock

Don't think about it,

Just jump off

I promise you it's soft

Try to be yourself

Try to be free

Find that independence - stop trying to be me

BEYOND THE GRAVE

Have you ever seen the moon half full?

Or an angel on a pier

Have you ever felt the wind of a bomb?

Or the end of every dripping tear

Have you ever watched the sun rise and fall?

Proving once more,

It will restart after all

She gave me life and I never realized

I gave her a commitment

I'd keep until I died

Love isn't about time

It's about what's kept inside

A no love words or acts could divide

Life is long-

At least a few good things are shown

With someone like you it's hard to be wrong

And God it's so true what they say:

These days aren't worth the price we paid"

Or are they?

I'd like to think so…

At any cost -

We had it all

Even if this moment is long since lost

Like warriors on an even more distant path

We will stand tall

Overcome them all

Jump the walls

Prolong the fall

Erase the pain that puts us at fault

We will be remembered by more than a name

Defined by the hyphen between dates

The grave of the brave

FAITH?

Believe

Believe

Believe

That is all we have to stand on

Determination

Perseverance

Achieving our goals

What drives us

Faith?

Believe

Believe

Believe

INTERPERTATION

Falling asleep,

Another dream

Babies cradle alone,

On the beach

The tiny hands,

Just out of reach

The currents strength

Captivating

My spirit cries!

Someone help

No one's around

No help now

I dive in,

Dazzling effort

I start to drown

Feet couldn't reach

The cradle vanished

I think it was me

THE TRIP

Step into me

See what I see The walls around us

Constrict then recede

The mouth of the snake

Beginning to bleed

The venom it carries

Penetrates and stings

Here is the notion of the fear it brings

The path I'm on

Not totally free

Constantly begging for more

Positive thinking - negative dreaming

The heart will constantly be wishing

Especially when this trip ends

My mind will be blown

Mystical Journeys,

Lead me to Rome

A horse that is pale

A "man" holding scales

A newborn "child"

No way to prepare

Is the Earth on fire

Or is this hell…

With one more sign left -

It's too early to tell

THE ANCIENT WITNESS

Sleep now in the meadow

A pasture free,

Imprisoned ghettos lingering

The smell was horrific,

Burning hair in the distance

A trick!

We were told to stay Gun shots were heard

At the instant,

Truths were hidden,

Alone in the pasture,

Appeared a young man

He was fleeing his burning village

His frightened face,

Who could forget the image?

I grimaced with him in pain

The western sky eclipsed his fears

The sun god was near

He witnessed the killing of innocence

Just as we had during those years

We did nothing to stop it…

A story was shared

Old and forgotten

Told by the ancient witness

THE GHETTO

In the ghetto police roam our neighborhoods

In the ghetto selling drugs are a way out

In the ghetto we have book scholars

In the ghetto we have street scholars

In the ghetto we have single parents

In the ghetto we don't have access to the same
resources as most

In the ghetto we don't have someone to protect us
from the police

In the ghetto your guilty until proven innocent

Why are things so different in the ghetto?

AND STILL WE RISE

Does my black skin offend you?

Why are you so scared?

Because we shine brighter than the sun

Lock us in chains and beat us

Like smoke still we rise

You want to see us defeated begging for mercy

But my pride and sense of worth won't let me die

Soaring higher than an eagle and still we rise

Love one another my brothers and sisters

Stop the cycle of poverty help your kids flourish

So when they have kids they will see the light
because even on the Darkest nights when hate is all
around look up to the sky and small And just like
the moon and still we rise

DIARY OF A DEAD MAN

Shelter me in the hands of fools

For I want to see something new

And shadowing stars chase nearby

I'll dream for a while,

What is it like to die

Along Martin Luther King's restless dreams

And Malcom X's dying screams

I wanted to be aware of God's requiem

Or at least,

What his plan was for me

 I died slowly and abruptly

Letting go of breathing uncontrollably

 I like to pretend I had a choice

As heartbeats began to void

I filled the new silence with a voice

"Where am I"

"Where did I go?"

These things I prayed someone to show

I had lost the war I've fought since birth

I am harmed by emotions' scarring hurt

Everyone does it son,

It's ok to lose

Smile while you're buried in a business suit

We all pretended like it's something we choose

I followed the shadow now in my mind

And prayed to God to have more time

My body failed me

As everything else

Leaving to early

As a sunset melts

I am alone as I was before

There are no more shadows

Before me on the floor

I only see the obscure things

No one has ever seen

And the spirits of the damned

Or angels feet

I am alone,

I am ALONE,

I am here forever

Forever gone…

Tomorrow I hope to awake to a kingdom

Promised by saints in my dying freedom

Though,

No one was here to comfort me

And why,

As the most uncertain time in my life,

I left terrified

There is a bitter feeling,

That no one can understand

Accept for the man

Where the tombstone stands

I love the honesty in a truthful date

Or inscrutable lines,

We tend to mistake,

As love divided by hate

And the wrong,

And the right,

And the dreams that kept you awake at night

These troubles

Now being more mature

I know this is only forever,

Forever for the impure

Are you finished yet, sir?

Or at least finished trying

This is your fate,

It comes with dying

There above you,

Your children are crying

And moving along,

A similar fate eying

Do you understand these things as true?

Because living for the dead is difficult for few

In death there are no misunderstandings

It was comical to ask a question in my waking

I understood things,

The things they were taking

And memories of them remembering

The only voices that drove me crazy

It is haunting to know you

caused pain

A permanent staining,

Or a museum painitng

They come to visit me and tell me things

I can only feel,

But I imagine their words

They are touching,

But make dying hard

Death is not dying until we're forgotten

And then there is jealousy,

You should be here with me!

We are both the same,

And both worth forgetting

There is no shame in this!

Death brings bliss,

And bliss brings madness

And madness

Only true madness

Brings silence to the tragic

I want to travel my lost loves heart

Or revisit a time in my life

Where I was innocent,

Nothing seemed more tragic than this

I found myself beginning to forget

The names of those that loved me,

And the tingle of a kiss

There is no destined moon for me anymore

There is no soul for me to adore

There is no friendship or heartache,

Or a life without God

Here I am stranded

Forced to move on

Or to stand still

Paint the painting backwards

So when it is placed in a mirror

It might reflect its master

I have forgotten my face

I have forgotten my eyes

I have forgotten my body

This is what it's like to die

Then there is absolute silence once again

I am comforted by no one

I am known by no one

Unless my past loves tend to dream

And meet me there against the stream

Do they want me to take a drink?

How strange

Do they not know?

I no longer thirst for anything

I comfort them though

And accept their offering

They smile and sooth my thoughts

Like doves getting lost

Building nest under a loft

Their offspring will be scurrying soon

And demons will cloud thoughts

As an infinite structure meets its down

They'll be joining me soon

Though in their youth

They'll feel there's no room

The wise will promise them

It is coming with time

Thoughts are beginning to cease now

I've analyzed it all

It has become quite the joke

When all loved ones fall

But they did not meet me

And they surely couldn't call

"Did you get my message on Facebook?"

"No, not at all,

This social life you speak of,

I am not involved."

This social life you speak of

Can you tell me more?

There are tons of laughing pictures

The communication was raptured

There was nothing more

I was speaking to myself

Imagining a little more

I imagined there were friends ,

And families with kids,

And pets in the background

Pissing on the ground,

Ironic,

In a way,

We all forget to say

The things we truly mean,

When we are approaching the grave

This generation is lovely,

Don't you think?

I expected nothing less

For them to be tagged on their feet

They left with a bang

Did they not?

But death in the same

In case you forgot

They could not beat me

And the disease

Of final words,

And lovely sanctuaries

To the end of time

And heavenly gates!

Our loved ones will be awake!

And still in love with us,

Despite their fate

Because everyone says,

It's a better place

This,

To me,

Angers the most

As it provokes animosity,

Between the dead and the Ghosts

Answers to questions are coming fast

As to why I'm here,

And how long this will last

What do I call this place?

As it is not heaven or hell

It is not anything,

But maybe a prison cell

Was I bad in life?

Or worse in death,

Did I owe my heavenly father,

A certain kind of debt?

I fear my situation is worse

Because I've been forgotten

Stuck between saints,

And the process of rotting

Though I'm unaware

It is hard not to stare

As it's the only sign of the world

Left to my care

Now I truly know the answers to my soul

Death is unbeatable,

It is not for show,

Death is hard for most

Though some will try to boast

"I ended up ending fine,

This is the life I chose."

But now I understand

Why I am here

I have done nothing in life,

I lived in fear

Death is the final thing we do

In order to understand

Life is to be lived,

And appreciated to the end

Life is the diary of a dead man

9 798739 189332